near
relations

BOOKS BY JOHN REIBETANZ

POETRY
Ashbourn (1986)
Morning Watch (1995)
Midland Swimmer (1996)
Near Finisterre (1996)
Mining for Sun (2000)
Near Relations (2005)

CRITICISM
The Lear World (1977)

near
relations

JOHN REIBETANZ

M&S

Library and Archives Canada Cataloguing in Publication

Reibetanz, John
Near relations / John Reibetanz.

Poems.
ISBN 0-7710-7355-0

I. Title.

PS8585.E448N44 2005   C811'.54   C2004-906722-2

We acknowledge the financial support of the Government of Canada through the Book Publishing Industry Development Program and that of the Government of Ontario through the Ontario Media Development Corporation's Ontario Book Initiative. We further acknowledge the support of the Canada Council for the Arts and the Ontario Arts Council for our publishing program.

The lyrics on page 37 are taken from "That Lucky Old Sun" by Beasely Smith and Haven Gillespie. Copyright © 1949 (Renewed 1977) EMI Robbins Catalog Inc. All Rights Controlled by EMI Robbins Catalog Inc. (Publishing) and Warner Bros. Publications Inc. (Print)   All Rights Reserved   Used by Permission WARNER BROS. PUBLICATIONS U.S. INC., Miami, FL. 33014

Text design by Sean Tai
Typeset in Minion by M&S, Toronto
Printed and bound in Canada

This book is printed on acid-free paper that is 100% recycled, ancient-forest friendly (100% post-consumer recycled).

McClelland & Stewart Ltd.
The Canadian Publishers
481 University Avenue
Toronto, Ontario
M5G 2E9
www.mcclelland.com

1 2 3 4 5   09 08 07 06 05

*To Julie, nearest
relation, heart's happiest
necessary song*

CONTENTS

III

near
relations

Spinner

Her eyes belong to no child. Moses
   looked through them, lenses branded
with the afterimage of God's fire,
   and saw his people's future
grow old under the weight of carved stone.
   Truth, Socrates knew through them,
comes home to port in a ship whose slack
   sail is the colour of death.

How old was she when Lewis Hine's lens
   caught her image in *Spinner*,
Cotton Mill? No veins, no wrinkles mar
   arms that brace her like an A
written in the narrow aisle between
   window and power loom. Is
her flat chest a sign of childhood or
   vestige of poor food, poor sleep?

Under a forehead smooth as marble
   unblinking eyes hold neither
sorrow's tears nor joy's, so full they are
   with knowing. They hold all words
that you might say, and deeper within
   they draw from some hidden well
the icy certainty that no words
   will make any difference.

She would not call it work, my sitting
    for hours staring at a point
below her intolerable gaze
    and above the soiled neckband
of undershirt that lines her collar,
    intent on catching from those
slightly pursed lips the unearthly thread
    of what she's about to say.

I

Lincoln Logs

Once upon a time. A six-year-old boy
    almost might be raising himself
from the waters of sleep, onto a beach
    made glass when a wave's sheet pulls taut.
His left arm props his torso, his legs (still
    sleeping?) trail behind like a seal's
footless, tapered shank. Almost. But the gloss
    this beach holds is the solid flow
of a waxed floor, and the boy's eyes – open,
    their own glitter fully wakened –
focus on his right hand about to crown
    an afternoon's labour. He holds
a wooden cube and sets the inverted
    carved V of its base in triumph
on a green cardboard roof: the log cabin
    has its chimney. He has built well,
linking the dovetailed, pencil-thick pieces
    of squared cedar, blocking out
the door and windows, even contriving
    an alcove where his frontiersmen
will hang their coonskin caps and long rifles.

There is so much he doesn't know. If his
    ignorance were a log, its weight
would crush him. He has no idea his mother,
    who reads *The Deerslayer* to him
while he builds, lives mostly in a country
    called madness, and her body will

spend the next two years in an asylum.
        He doesn't know that the gleaming
linoleum floor will fail to hold him,
        giving way to spare-room sofas,
basement daybeds, fold-ups, as he's shunted
        from hand to ever-more-remote
hand in the family bucket brigade.
        He won't realize for decades
that the last few distant uncles and aunts
        are paid strangers, and even the
logs' honest "Lincoln" is a hollow pun.

Yet, he doesn't need your pity or mine.
        He sees the mirroring water
doubling the cabin's height is Glimmerglass,
        the lake where Deerslayer held off
marauding Hurons in his log refuge.
        He senses it's in the reflected
cabin that Cooper's "dark chest" holds the secret
        of who we are. He is the boy
who will open the cardboard cylinder
        of Lincoln Logs in every room
he lands in, building his cabin again
        and again. The boy who floats
in his white jersey like smoke pluming from
        the chimney, or like the genie
of a tale he's read on his own, set free
        from a bottle that can't hold him.
Who will learn – or does he need to learn? –
        the answer to a nightmare is

to build a cabin on a sheet of water,
    sinking the pencil-thick supports
into the fathomless centre of a dream.

TORTOISE FAMILY CONNECTIONS

1.
More relentlessly than anything else
you know, except for life, the sun moves on.

Slower than the slowest tortoise, it bores
a course through free air as unvarying

as if it threaded a steel shaft. You think
nothing so premeditated could be

kind, you're right: look wide-eyed at its face and
it will eat out your eyes. Every night, like

clockwork, it withdraws into a cold, black,
spotted shell where breath starves. Creatures shorter-

lived than the sun, warm-blooded, move faster,
trying to pack the most motion into

their contracting footfalls, desperate to
outrun the jaws' toothless, fleshless axe.

2.
The shaft of light works its way tortoiselike
across the snapshot, metes out pulse as if

the old man's veins coursed quicksilver. He
sits like a tipped-back tortoise wedged between

the pillows of a gilded Chippendale
loveseat, the dome of his underbelly

lapped by pinstripe trousers almost up to
his chest. It's Christmas, the unlidded box

of handkerchiefs reveals – still swaddled in
giftwrap on the side table, the top one's

silk monogram *CR* smartly centred,
bordered by a ribbon of smoke rising

from the ashtray-cradled Cuban. In light's
most intense glare, his tortoise eyes are ice.

3.
He would, later that same winter, withdraw
with wife and Chippendales and Aubusson

(three pale rosettes from the corner of which
his feet half cover) into a marqueed,

doormanned apartment, selling this house with
its costly roof and furnace, leaving his son

the bills. That son would work two jobs (fatigue
nearly yielding a hand up to the jaws

of a punch-press), pawn his heirloom watch
next Christmas for his son's first bicycle,

never speak to his father again
and never quite believe he could be loved

by a child who worked this story out too late:

poor gift too slow come from my tortoise hand.

Ear and Eye (1)

"The hearing ear, and the seeing eye, the Lord
hath made even both of them." – *Proverbs 20:12*

Since he and the man he shouted them at
and that man's daughter are long dead,
you'll have to take my word that the words
"Daddy, Daddy!" once were uttered

by a little boy of colour
running in a flock of paler children
(my mother and aunt among them) behind
my maternal grandfather

Martin Hanley who, one Friday
evening, coming home from work
with a pocketful of nickels,
doled them out as ice-cream money

to the kids who followed him;
through cries of "Daddy, Daddy!"
breath made them one family
for a breath (the way stadium

cheering makes one of a crowd)
to the delight of Martin Hanley,
a single mother's only child
who, far more than money, valued

even for a moment feeling
father to so many children
(never having enough of his own)
and whose ear prized most of all

the "Daddy, Daddy!" of this child –
great-grandson of the field workers
a grandfather Martin never knew
had worked and fought beside

so that on this Friday evening
(while his Irish eyes smiled
at the sound) the air might hold
adopted oneness raised to song.

SHUCKS

O where are the chortles of yesteryear?
Out of breath – since no one chortles now –
they've shrivelled to dry scratchmarks on the pages
of newsprint, casket-stacked in library basements.

When I was nine or ten, chortles chortled
from everybody's den – which we called parlour,
a room grown scarce since wedded to funerals.
With their first cousins, chuckles, chortles rose

in small balloons from Little Orphan Annie,
Dagwood and Blondie, and with harrumphs and guffaws
hovered over the fez of Major Hoople
who has also gone the way of all chortles.

I heard them in the parlour of my best friend,
Joseph Palumbo. While we sat on the floor
playing Monopoly, they rose over the tent
of *Telegram* atop his father's armchair.

Mr. Palumbo was an educated man
who set type at our local newspaper
and loved to read out bits from the comics,
curiosities from *Ripley's Believe It or Not*,

and sometimes, when the mood offered, swatches
of his favourite poet, Edna St. Vincent Millay.
That's where I first encountered the lore of "lore"
(rhyming with "ardour") and heard "clarions,"

which stopped sounding when Mr. Palumbo's job
forsook him for a typesetting machine.
Month by month under the silent tent
he shrivelled, until his heart, aching to steal

his life out of the frail shell he'd become,
broke free. I like to think of Mr. Palumbo
resettled in a world of abandoned words,
keeping house with Edna St. Vincent Millay.

He puts his paper down and asks would she
like to try a Charleston or a Lindy,
some steps long since shucked off by mortal feet.
Both rise and, chortling, trip the light fantastic.

What Just Was

The road to school was the closest I came to death:
darkness welled and clotted, a tar pool
you could just by some miracle breathe through.

Michaela had come closer. Her father, hoping
to sleep his way out of debt, turned on the gas
and scuttled himself, his wife, their mortgaged house.

Now she lived with her aunt on my side of town.
We met mornings to walk to school, running
where the road ran through the cemetery.

It wasn't just the shuddering of branches
around and above: drawn down between
high banks, the road caved in to rooted gloom,

and behind the iron fence, a downward pull
levelled the raised loaves of fresh plots
and sucked older headstones deep into turf –

something under the groomed nap seething
with a will to extinguish. On the walk home, high sun
broke the spell enough for us to risk

slipping in past a bowed iron fencebar
to take a shortcut over gravelled footpaths
to another gap at the far end. We crossed

a stream you couldn't see from the road, feet
drumming the floorboards of the wooden bridge
to send a heartbeat through the mute village

of stonebound, narrow lanes.
                                        Feeling bolder
one spring afternoon (the leaves still buds
letting light flood through), we paused on the bridge

and looked down from the highest point of the arch.
The stream ran swollen, glossy brown except
where rocks turned up tufted white patches

and, right below us, where a hidden whirlpool
of strong current spun under the bridge
and flung out water-diamonds from a pinwheel

just beyond sight. We hunched beneath the rails
and leaned over. Schooling up, circling
one of the creosoted pillars,

what looked like fat minnows bobbed and swayed,
riding the current. We looked again: not minnows.
Both too shy to say what we both saw –

the school of condoms: some flat, some distended
with water, all dancing – we watched in silence,
red-faced with shame, and with an awkward sense

of something stirring within us like what stirred
below: a pulse, rising from our own dark parts,
that would grow strong enough to carry us

clear out of childhood. Unforgettable
dance, unthinkable to talk about
as her lost parents, an obscenity

we bowed to every afternoon that spring
in the same hushed, innocent homage.
                                    Nothing
earthshaking came of it – soon we went on

to different schools, lost touch – nothing except
the going on itself, a flowing through earth's
nothing on something human that just was.

Night Thoughts

Sometimes when essays I've been grading all day wake me in the middle
      of the night,
their lines of brassy split infinitives and thumping sentence
      fragments parading
around the same small track like a high-school marching band whose
      morning practices
make the whole neighbourhood thoroughly sick of Christmas by
      late October,
I think with envy of my father-in-law who, untenured and unprivileged,
rose early every weekday to do all the cooking for the little lunchroom
      he ran.

I envy his mornings spent among the surenesses of milk, butter, flour,
his never having to tell the bread to be more specific or the tea more clear,
his providing certain nourishment for those he served, and being able
      to watch
as they took it all in and made it part of themselves, licking every
      last crumb
of wisdom from his forks. Most of all I envy one particular winter night
when he looked at the clock and mistook 12:20 for 4:00, his usual
      wake-up hour.

Flipping off the alarm so it wouldn't wake his wife, he rose,
      washed, dressed,
and walked through the still sleeping streets to the kitchen door of
      Yonge Lunch,
where he struck a match, as usual, to guide the key into the lock.
      Stepping inside,

under fluorescent dawn he started his day – hands rolling, shaping,
    setting pies to bake,
then the stew's bladework assembled for the daily special, then pots
    of coffee –
wordlessly conducting in the lunchroom air his silent symphony of aromas.

When he was just beginning to wonder why daybreak was so long
    in coming,
Constable Reilly, also in wonderment, used his passkey to come in at the
    front door.
Their misapprehensions cleared up, the two of them sat and ate slices
    from the sun
of a lemon pie, and toasted its early rising with fresh coffee: real food to
    savour, when my
night kitchen serves up only bowls of dense comma splice noodled
    with dangling
participle, plates of rancid cliché not even a hungry policeman
    would go for.

The Kermes-Berry

"Hang there like fruit, my soul,
Till the tree die" – *Cymbeline*

1.
Lunch is sandwiches on the road to Stratford,
but "Fresh-Picked Berries" means a sweet detour.
The farmer gossips about his Mennonite
pickers. One of them naps among the baskets –

2.
"cocooned," we would say – in her father's windbreaker
here at the edge of the field. Yet, if that word
slid down her ear's coil (miniature of
the pod her sleeping body keeps) and woke her,
she could not take it in. "Capullo" might
stir up dream-moultings from a Mexican phase
of her short life, but only "Puppe" can
unseal her eyelid's chrysalis with light.

"Puppe": Old German lozenge, carried on
tongues of Mennonite migrants overland
across three continents. Puppe curls under
Maria's arm – not "pupa" or "cocoon"
to her, but "dolly," in this Scotch pine's shade
where a morning picking strawberries in full sun
has stained the child's cheeks red as Puppe's cloth ones
while her mother scrubs sheets stained with darker red.

3.
Last night Maria lost a sister rocked
in her mother's body on the long drive north.
This morning her father settled the stillbirth in
deep shade beyond the field the migrants pick.

4.
Maria's shade is kinder, waterthinned
and honeycombed with light. She will break out
while we sit shuttered at the matinee,
and flit around the field. Will her wings
ever lift her above the tribal orbit
of pain emerging from girlhood's split cocoon?
For now she sleeps, Puppe's twin, knowing
light only as light touches the sealed fruit.

She does not know the long journey "cocoon"
travelled through ancient ignorance: how the Greeks
found, hanging in clusters from scarlet oaks,
something they took for fruit and named "kokkos,"
the kermes-berry. Slaves pounded red juice from it
to dye the Roman "coccinum" – crimson robe
of those who never knew the kermes-berry
was the dried body of a female insect.

5.
Some of the harvest picked by these small fingers
will make the rounds among our easy chairs
tonight, as we sit discussing Shakespeare,
the berries reddening our fluent tongues.

To Cathy

It was such a surprise hearing from you
out of the blue (grey, actually, with white
    piping running along the top). Never
expecting stowaways in my underwear,
    I jumped when something like a dappled wing
fluttered out from the shorts I was unwrapping.
    On it, your printed lines and written name.
Wonder what kind of girl would sneak notes into
    the folds of a man's underwear. Do they
call you "forward" there in Truro? – it's a place
    small enough for a "reputation" to
sink a girl's hopes of marriage. Signing just
    "Cathy" to a stranger would seem brazen,
and the jaunty way your crossed "t" sidles up
    to your "h" might raise suspicions. Did this
start with your calling grownups by their first names?
    And now you make these furtive liaisons –
hundreds, it must be, every day, for if I
    found two (the other pair also had its
billet-doux holed up in the flap), how many
    other men's briefs are you fingering? Do
you do it for minimum wage, just for
    the thrill? Or are you – I'm wary of those
hints about "comfort and style" and "exclusive
    fabrics" – after my money?
                                    Probably
neither. Let me write, this time. Jumping ship at
    sixteen from a school going nowhere, you

landed at the Stanfield's factory. Now, years
    later, you slip these out like castaway
notes in bottles after you've "personally
    inspected" each garment to make sure it
meets those high standards that, you underline, make
    Stanfield's famous. And even if you've grown
so expert you just go through the motions and
    let your thoughts drift off, there must be mornings
when the stack of white squares towers, and you
    wonder how can there be enough Cathy
to launch the whole day's worth of Cathy bits,
    and how much you will be at the day's end.

Ear and Eye (2)

No words here, no sounds.
Only the eye takes in what looks
at first to be the roofed stands
of a stadium – filled racks

stretching in two banked layers, broken
only by support posts pitched
from ground to roof – but what on closer
view is too small for a sitting

gallery, each level scarcely
a metre high, more like the stalls
of a fruit stand; yet a spectral,
retinal stadium persists

because such intense scrutiny
stares from the upper layer of
this Cambodian Museum
of Genocide, where bald spectators,

having long lost their senses (sheer
bone where the ears opened; holes
where the eyes have disappeared)
have been placed in ascending rows

matching the arm and leg bones
set beneath them so exactly
that the viewer half sees, half hopes
to see the skulls connected to

the bones below, necks hidden by
the upper shelf front; yet if that
were so, these neighbouring heads would be
different – skin dark or pale, hair short

or long – but they are all one shape,
one shade, skulls purged of everything
that parts. Here sight, bereaved, calls up
one family from the ruins of song.

II

No, she's not the woman we're driving south to visit, but I can't get her image out of my mind. Did something in the acid-edged air print it there, like a laser engraving? Maybe it was just how quickly it wiped out every-thing else, the lightning strike of an invading force – when I had thought of myself as the invader this time.

An invader supported by a minivan full of children: ours, Canadian-born, free of the baggage that came with my largely American childhood. We have brought our own air with us over the border, sweet with the baskets of fresh peaches and early apples that will turn the drive into one long picnic. Or a movie: we'll sit in our glass bubble while the travelogue unreels. But now, without warning, the screen goes dark. And we're breathing poison. Out of the winding green solitude of the Alleghenies, Johnsonburg has struck, a huddle of blackened buildings and crumbling asphalt at the core of a steep, tree-banked valley. The yellow ooze from half a dozen brick chimneys has seeped into our little steel and glass stronghold and set our eyes streaming. Coughing, clearing throats, reaching for tissues, we feel held for ransom by the traffic light that stops us for no visible reason: no people, no cars, nothing but fumes and soot-caked walls. When the light finally changes, I gun the motor to speed us up the narrow street that leads out of the valley. That's when I notice her, the only living person evident in this man-made moonscape.

Ahead on our right, proceeding casually down the sidewalk into the gloom we're breathless to climb out of, a woman pushes a stroller past an abandoned Woolworth's store. Though the day is hot, she and her child both seem terribly underclothed in their white T-shirts and pastel shorts, vulner-able. Their faces are equally white and unlined, but hers has the broader smile. She smiles ahead without seeing us, as if she were part of a painting beaming out at the world in general, oblivious to the hook that holds her. Her eyes wear the wide geniality of a mannequin in a display window. The child, in contrast, focuses pointedly at and through me from under her pink sunbonnet, as if her eyes were both sharper and older than her mother's. The child's eyes seem to gather the blackened walls and the bitter fumes and aim them at me, not from animosity – her brow is serene, unclenched – but with the steadiness of a fountain guiding furious water through its stone aperture, as a kind of gift: welcome back to your birthright.

Yes, I have seen these eyes before. In the oldest photograph I have of my mother. At seven or eight, she sits straightbacked in a straightbacked chair, her hands folded – as children never do unless they're told to – on a little desk. The hands signal compliance, but the eyes flash a different message, one that I heard decades later from her lips. They speak of how she was sent down to Sister Superior's office that morning for "telling stories," made to own up that she wasn't a princess in disguise, that her grandmother really was her grandmother and not an old family servant, that she would not be reclaimed when her true parents returned from their voyage around the world. The eyes also hold her knowledge that her parents' marriage has fallen apart and that she is now living in her grandmother's flat, across the street from this new school, while her mother scrubs floors in the rectory.

And the Johnsonburg mother's eyes? I've seen them too, also in an image of my mother, but not a photograph. I've seen them countless times in nightmares and in waking up from nightmares when I've tried not to see them, ever since the time they stared out at me (aged six) from the stretcher that carried her away for two years (which was forever then) after her suicide attempt.

Corrosive as the Johnsonburg fumes, an old, long-unfamiliar feeling invades the space at the back of my thoughts: the same sense of helplessness that clung to me during the years of race riots and Vietnam, and that I left behind me by moving north. Our minivan climbs up out of the valley, but the Johnsonburg woman and her child roll obsessively through my mind. Back in the motherland.

$\sim$

We are driving south so I can pay one last visit to my mother, who is dying of bone cancer. We have chosen a roundabout route, partly to put some sugar coating of holiday on the journey for the kids, partly to defer what will be painful. Our journey will shape a large hook down through Pennsylvania and Maryland into Washington, then curve up to the barb that awaits me in New Jersey. We make our first stop at Gettysburg, maybe in response to some of the nightmare visions of wars on foreign soil that have troubled this summer. Or perhaps to encounter an enlarged, catastrophic version of my own inner war and the personal act of secession that brought me to Canada in my twenties.

Whatever we've come to see, it's hard to find. The battlefield lies under a heavy fog, offering everywhere the same foreshortened scene of grass and granite monument, like scattered pieces of a Stonehenge puzzle. The fog delights the guide, who steers us through a two-hour tracing of the legendary three days of troop movements and confrontations. It's just the way it would have looked, he tells us, under the smoke from thousands of Union and Confederate guns. "Confusing" comes to my mind, but his vocabulary runs more to words like "ennobled," "gallantry," and "hallowed," interspersed grotesquely with statistics itemizing cannon, shells, amputations, and dead horses.

Our very Canadian nine-year-old asks a question I only think, but that he's brave enough to say: How many men took advantage of the confusion to slip away? To a saner world, he might have added. The mildly shocked response – with a look that questions my parenting – is that nobody ran away from Gettysburg. Everybody knew what was at stake. It was a privilege to play such a key role in their country's history, and they knew it. By manoeuvring the small talk, I learn that our guide is himself a veteran. He fought in a more recent war in his country's history, one with no battlefield tours. Leaving, he presses on us a copy of the Civil War magazine *Blue & Gray* like an evangelist pushing Bibles. The magazine's motto is "For those who still hear the guns." As I watch him disappear into the fog, I think about the union, or the confederacy, of fog and deafness.

It has become easier for me to avoid brooding over my own decision not to hear the guns of the 1970s, because history has been sympathetic to the evasions of that decade, and because a nomadic childhood left me with far shallower roots in America than those I've put down in Canada. Much harder to put out of my mind, especially on this journey, is the deeply personal turmoil stirred up by the guide's comparison of fog to smoke.

"Your mother's in a fog again," my father tells me as I arrive home from grade eight that afternoon, surprised to see him there and not at work. I know quite well that "in a fog" is his euphemism for "withdrawn into paranoid depression," but for a moment something – my instinct for evasion? – makes me take his words as plain description. For she sits at the kitchen table in her own fog of smoke, mechanically puffing on a cigarette with one hand while writing with the other. If I speak to her, she will not hear. This act of secession, foreshadowed for weeks in brief but frightening lapses of attention, will remove her from the republic of our family for another two years. For, behind the shifting grey veils, battle plans are unfolding; her quivering pencil is making a list of traitors that includes my aunts, my uncles, my father and me.

Years later, when I took up smoking at university, I was overcome with nausea if I ever lit up while writing. At the time, I had no idea why.

~

Bright sunlight sees us into Washington next morning: expanses of Maryland countryside, deep green even at the end of the dry summer, give way to manicured lawns, tennis clubs, and other icons of suburban affluence. These in turn give way to more commercial buildings, and then the road itself starts to give way. Unpatched cracks, potholes that could swallow whole wheels, tussocks of asphalt – random speed bumps – make it impossible to drive anything like the posted limit. In sympathy, the stores and houses along the road become equally dilapidated: broken windows, boarded windows, half-demolished walls like abandoned Lego games of colossal bored children. What armies have been moiling across *this* battlefield? Their casualties are lying on bus-stop benches and shored against lampposts and storefronts. Those with open eyes stare menacingly or stupidly. Still hearing the guns?

We decide to spend the afternoon at the Museum of Air and Space, suddenly feeling much in need of both, and pause at our hotel only long enough to check in. In a manoeuvre I will understand only later, the manager urges us to park our car in the driveway for now, rather than move it down to the underground garage, and to take a cab for as much sightseeing as we can fit in. I take his advice. The Washington streets are better left to more seasoned drivers and stronger-built springs.

The Museum of Air and Space was built with the vaultlike strength of the pyramids. Its vast Space entombs not pharaohs but machines, from the Wright Brothers' first plane to the space shuttles of the 1980s. It is a shrine for the gods of American technology, and its altars offer formidable proof of the dominance of those gods over the twentieth century. Even the cafeteria is a technological wonder, marshalling brightly dressed slave-armies of tourists – this is the most visited museum in the world – with admirable speed, and directing them to tables under a great glass and steel canopy. "Wow" seems to be the appropriate password here. It comes spontaneously to our lips throughout the afternoon.

But the most exciting part of the day awaits me in the evening. The phone rings in our hotel room just as the kids are getting ready for bed: the night manager asks me to move the car underground; the driveway space is now needed by a van too big for the garage. I meet him at the front desk and am impressed, naively, by his offer to accompany me. But he makes it from the hotel door to the car in an Olympic sprint, with me doing my best to keep up. Then together we drive out into the Washington night.

As we move down the block, the only light comes from our headlights and one feeble streetlamp. Where has the city gone? Through the gloom, I can pick out little knots of people along the sidewalk every fifteen or twenty feet, crouching or kneeling, very intent on whatever they are doing. Small fires flicker from the centres of these groups. The scene is tribal and pastoral, with the low, throbbing growl of transistor radios – all tuned to different stations, it seems – heard through the closed car window as appropriate audio accompaniment.

We turn into a cavelike laneway. Down it, two wheel ruts stretch ahead through chunks of concrete and brick, shards of amber glass, drifts of newsprint. Only the sides of this tunnel are intact, an expanse of solid brick walls and battered metal doors. Through a couple of the doors, tilted open, I catch glimpses of those Halloweenish circles I saw on the sidewalks. At last, the tunnel swerves and descends. We stop at a small speaker midway down the ramp. I give my name and room number. A portcullis rises, then swiftly clatters down behind us. In the mirrored wall of the elevator back upstairs, I see that my shirt is soaked through.

As I try to drift into sleep, the long day simplifies itself into a few long-familiar images. The small fires and radio noise of the street coalesce into the rosy glow of the dial on my first transistor radio – itself once a marvel of technology – which I listen to under my bed. When I lie on my back, the slats and webbing on the underside of the box-spring canopy my little tunnel like the museum roof. I am seven or eight, as old as my mother was when her parents split up. Mine haven't, but they quarrel constantly after I'm in bed, so I take refuge under it. My main source of comfort is the radio, especially when Jean Shepherd comes on after eleven and tells stories about his childhood in the steel towns of Indiana. I've heard his style from friends, but never before from a grownup: the fresh, rude words that adults forget they've ever used, the sense of other kids as fellow conspirators, the fears that seem both silly and overpowering at the same time – like when Schwarz runs away from home because movers are coming to take away the fridge behind which he's been pitching the despised tomato slices from his sandwich every day. Best of all, Shepherd tells his stories like one of those jugglers who spins a plate on a stick and keeps adding extra sticks and plates until surely the whole gyrating contraption will collapse. By then, the outbursts from the room next door have usually subsided, and the radio's little red light is blurring, dancing, but I will not crawl into bed until, red, green, blue, yellow – the whole rainbow of characters and story lines hovering in the air – miraculously, he catches them all at the last minute and whispers them into place.

~

A day of white and black.

It's best to see the Capitol early in the morning, before the crowds arrive. But it's also just as intimidating as the hotel's back alley, in a daylight kind of way. The building towers numbingly. Like bleached bones of a reassembled dinosaur skeleton, the facade's columns stretch on forever with stupefying redundancy. Looking up at the cataract of white stone steps, I feel as if I've just downed Alice's miniaturizing potion, but the pure American tourists seem thrilled rather than chilled, reverent and uncritical. Inside, they do not giggle as my children do at the rotunda ceiling painting of George Washington in apotheosis, flanked by adoring angels, his hand fixed in a papal salute. Nor do they find it odd that the Representatives, those hard-working voices of the people, have no desks in their chamber, unlike the more patrician Senators. Or that, just blocks from this panelled and carpeted citadel of government "by the people, for the people," the people are living in hovels, on a diet of poverty and cocaine. Isolated, I turn to my guidebook: "If this Nation has an ennobling shrine, the Capitol is it." We're supposed to genuflect, not evaluate.

Our little band of irreverent Canadian pilgrims is much happier with the scale of our next shrine, as early afternoon finds us in a small museum, the Phillips Collection, before one painting in particular: Renoir's *Luncheon of the Boating Party*. It occupies the place of a hearth in one room of the old house, an ample, light-filled hearth, and it shows a much more lavish picnic than the one of apples and peaches that began our trip. But "shows" is too neutral and distanced a word: the scale and warmth of this painting *invite* us to a picnic. Around the fruits and wines of the table we pull up chairs and join Renoir's animated circle of friends.

The very tones of their conversation, its eager, lyric ups and downs, flow around us through the bright colours and varied textures, until we wonder if our senses are up to taking it all in. The room shimmers with the uncontainable liveliness of the best comedy – appropriately, since the painting is in fact a little play staged by Renoir: he assembled the actors, costumes, and props. And though she sits to one side and looks at her little dog rather than at us, we have no doubt who the heroine is. Aline Charigot was eventually to become Renoir's wife and the mother of his children. When he painted her here at age twenty-one, she seemed hopelessly remote: knowing that he could not support a family, he would soon break off their relationship. We see her through his eyes, the only character dressed in inky black – in contrast to the radiance of white shirts and tablecloth around her. Yet, the black dress is itself radiant, and is fringed with red (matching the flowers in her sun-yellow hat) and with foaming white lace. Like all great comedies, this painting roots its joy in awareness of pain, the darkness intensifies its light. We face the correspondences between the bright, flushed faces and the shining, perishing fruit and delight in them all the more.

After this French excursion, we go Stateside again for our last stop of the day, the Museum of American History. History may have its blind spots, but it acknowledges – as Air and Space did not – the black tragedy at the heart of the Union. An exhibit on early America recreates the culture and conditions of the slaves. This place of suffering and heartbreak is the day's most moving shrine. We tour recreations of the "dependencies," as they were called, at places like Mount Vernon: slave quarters, out of sight from the main house, little more than brick caves. Their inadequate hearths are sadly reminiscent of those little sidewalk fires near our hotel, direct descendants in a long chain of deprivation. Washington's will gave his slaves their freedom, but his wife's will didn't free hers, and many black families were split up in the distribution of assets at her death. So the father of his

36

country unwittingly fathered an early version of the impoverished, single-parent misery that still burdens the city bearing his name.

As we march through American history into the Civil War, images of one representative figure in particular record the impact of slavery and its aftermath on white America. In chronologically arranged paintings and photographs of Lincoln, the topography of his face resists all attempts to smooth out deepening rifts and clear away thickening shadows. A tragic landscape, it registers the immense personal costs of the brutal war that had become glorious statistics for our Gettysburg guide. The last few images are harrowing, Lincoln's face becoming its own death mask as the lightless eyes withdraw into their caves and the blotched skin dries into glazed earthenware.

Just when our eyes can bear no more, our ears come to the rescue. Rising out of despair comes music – rag, blues, jazz, rock – the soul of this nation, its most cherished cultural gift to the rest of the world. We listen to the scratchy early recordings of Robert Johnson interrogating his guitar, and grief pours from it transformed into beauty. "Up in the mornin' / Out on the job," sings Louis Armstrong. "Dear Lord above," he asks, "can't you know I'm pining, / Tears all in my eyes," but he is asking in song, in a voice that seems carried away in wonder at its own deep richness. Here, at the dark centre of this city of granite bones, is living beauty, singing in inexplicable harmony with life's pain.

On this last night in Washington, song harmonizes with the personal and immediate pain that will occupy all my thoughts tomorrow, and takes the place of sleep. Jean Shepherd introduced me to storytelling, yes, but it was my mother's voice that first gave me song. Song, and the uses of song. I see her at the kitchen table – incredibly, she must have been just a few years older than Aline Charigot in Renoir's painting – singing while folding laundry or whisking eggs. In the five or six precarious years between her first breakdown and her second, as I half-sensed then and realize now, song let her breathe the demons out, before they grew too strong and pulled her back into their world again. Like Robert Johnson and Louis Armstrong, she sang mostly the songs of an oppressed people – in her case the Irish forebears of her mother and father. Roddy McCorley faces death heroically, Molly Malone pines away tragically, in ballads that drum or lilt pain into melody. Reliving their hurts in song, making lyric wholes out of their fragmented lives, the woman her parents named Veronica Leonora Frances Joan Hanley sang her own hurt life into beauty, even as I try to do now in sounding out her name.

~

The next day leaves my children happier – and I'm deeply grateful for that – than it leaves me. In preparation for our visit, my father and the visiting nurse have staged their version of Renoir's little show: my mother's wasted body is hidden under striped pink sheets and makeup, and her pain is masked with morphine. The conversation is all us and is ebullient: what the kids have seen and enjoyed in our travels, what we'll be doing when we get home. And when everyone else is ushered out and I am left alone with her for a few minutes, it's evident that the person I have come to see is absent: the sedated eyes looking out at me are those of the Johnsonburg mother, not her all-seeing, all-feeling daughter. Why does this bother me so much? Do I want my mother to be in pain? Surely I only want communication, closure, nothing more.

When I lean over to kiss her I am overwhelmed by a sense that this is not my mother. Her breath lacks the perfume of the familiar cigarette smoke. And now a voice long-buried – hidden much deeper than my mother's disease – rises up and shouts in my ear, yes! I do want you to suffer. The little boy is abandoned again. And unlike his friend Joseph Palumbo, whose father dies and never comes back, this little boy is doomed to repeated departures and returns. He will express bewildered happiness at each reunion ("You used to be fatter" is all I said at the first one, or so I was told), but all the time a little boy within him will be glaring at her through the fog of his own anger. Plotting to get even by – yes, it's finally clear now as we drive home after the last goodbye – his own act of abandonment, leaving

38

the motherland forever. Politically, that may have been a tactical with-
drawal, but personally it was a little boy's retaliation. For wasn't I her most
heartfelt song, her fresh white piece of paper, her story of the future? And I
could prove it, to myself if to no one else, by causing a pain that the part of
me not still a child can only hope has been eased by the palliative of time.

~

I am back home in Canada now, not in the now of my writing but in the now of writing it. After my mother's death, my father has forwarded some possessions that he thinks I might like to have. One of them is a small brown photograph album I've never seen before; it must have been buried away for years. Most of the snapshots seem to have been taken when my mother was thirteen, right after her mother had remarried, and they record the holiday that the stepfather gave his new wife and her two daughters. I keep coming back to one photo of my mother on a swing. She wears a white dress and white stockings, and she flies straight toward the camera with the happiest look I've ever seen on her face. Her wide open eyes sparkle, and her round open mouth, like a chorister's on a Christmas card, shows that she's singing. In ten years, her mother and stepfather will both be dead, she will have run off to a convent and tried unsuccessfully to turn herself into a nun, and she will be about to embark on a long but stormy marriage to the man who became my father. But in the perpetual now of the photograph, she sings.

I can never hear her singing, but I can fill the silence and the absence with song. Song brings consolation, but it never falsifies or attempts to cancel the loss by claiming substantiality. It floats in the air, lighter than a girl on a swing. It is breath, story's whitest dress. Song is my motherland, both my earliest home, a gift from her, and the adopted country where I choose to live.

39

III

It was *really there*, Ted swears — he makes his living visiting schools
and children's libraries, telling stories (and the word brands him
a professional liar, the brand-name recognition surviving since
Plato) — he swears it was, somewhere along the highway that ran
elevated, above the level of the tarred flat roofs of his childhood —
despite the fact that in fifty years he hasn't revisited those
lanes of crumbling asphalt trembling on rusted metal pillars:

the blocked-off beginning of an exit ramp that curved and yawned,
    arching
its back over a hundred feet of air to end like a story
broken off. The uncompleted ramp could go no farther.
Waiting to be traced like the dotted line in a colouring book, its flightpath
led to the side of a warehouse, and would have hit the windowless wall
where a row of yellow bricks interrupted the red facade to tell how,
inside, the ceiling of the third story met the floor of the fourth.

Decades later, he found in a book that a house's levels were called
stories because in ancient buildings rows of sculpted narrative
ran along the window lines. But Ted grew up in a bookless
house, no storerooms filled with words to furnish imagination's
bare rooms — so he raided that red brick warehouse for stories.
Once his eye had traced the ramp out past where it ended, once
he'd laid a pavement on the air, he found it an easy leap

to follow the roadway through and beyond the brick wall, tunnelling
and bridging landscapes that took shape to answer the asphalt tongue's
longing. Sometimes the road narrowed and climbed between stone ramparts
of a mountain fortress where he and his outlaw band hid out for years,
sometimes it plunged so deep the asphalt softened in earth's heat
and melted, baring the golden streets of a lost underground city.
No matter where the road led, it always began where the ramp, ending,

freed him from the metal rule of the guardrails, the way the taut strings
of his guitar throw up a flightpath of song from the bridge.
A building, Ted tells the children – strumming favourite conundrums –
    is really
always a-building, always relating stories; and the stillest road
will always be running by it. When he tells his stories, facts
open like exit ramps in the minds of his hearers, and what is real
lifts as what it's been since long before Plato: story, realized.

EXTENSION COURSES

Call them stupid, but his neighbours both knew their needs,
and those needs were huge: Pete Bodman's upstairs neighbour's
driftwood-grey hulk of a German shepherd, Lucky,
and his downstairs neighbour's enormous unnamed cello.

Stupid because, in the first place, nobody smart
would have chosen to live among their tenement's
echoing, nest-riddled walls – barracks where armies
of roaches bivouacked between nightly manoeuvres.

In the second place, neither neighbour could afford
to feed such large mouths. Lucky ate more than Carol
Torkelson's three kids, while the cello swallowed
Ida Lobalsamo's pension in taxi fares.

All this happened in a world of great stupidity
(Carol a mother on the run and not just
head of a single-parent family,
Ida a lonely eccentric, not an original),

yet Pete, the machinist on the floor between,
thanks to his neighbours, learned of other worlds.
A schoolhouse bell of sidewalk-hardened footpads
ringing the metal treads of the stairs would fetch him

out to the landing, where Lucky paused to be stroked:
under his fur, ribs worked a profound bellows,
and from his tongue's pink ledge a silver trickle
dripped like water from an underground spring.

To pet Lucky was to learn what luck could be –
fleet, but also muscular and deep-chested,
sinews meshing in faultless harmony.
The machinist touched the knowledge Carol Torkelson

needed to have beside her, and every night
he could hear the great dog settle overhead,
spiralling, nesting at the foot of Carol's bed.
Then, as his ear settled into the pillow,

another lesson rose from below to meet it.
Where Ida's bow sobbed against the strings,
a sparrow in slow motion took her grief
and winged it upward, freeing it from her.

Needing – more than sleep, more than sleep partners –
the soothing rhythm whose consolation became
that bird in flight singing along her nerve-ends,
she fell asleep with the cello between her knees.

And night after night, the machinist's room was visited
by a character born of both his neighbours' needs.
Both furred and feathered, it rose from its nest,
and he climbed on its back and rode out past the stars.

THE BIRDS OF THE AIR HAVE NESTS

You tell me why a swallow's nest should be
the one sign of triumph in a scene
filled with the presence and the handiwork
of the planet's highest form of life.

Pouch of dried mud, dingy sconce, plastered
to the bricks under the eaves. Across the street,
the abandoned factory's white facade towers
like an ocean liner moored along the sidewalk.

It will take ingenious demolition
to bring that down, but the sweep of a broom would be
enough to dislodge the swallow's nest and leave it
rubble under the P&H Lunchroom sign.

As Hilda would do, if she had time these days
to notice it. (As some kids passing by
did with a hockey stick early this spring,
before the swallows built it all over again.)

Yet, since the plant's closing and Peter's stroke,
she tells the few customers left – as if to scare
them off too – she's been cook, waitress, dishwasher,
all with him more trouble than a baby.

He can hear her, and knows she knows he can.
With his good hand he trawls a dishcloth over
unused back tables. The limp foot scuffs the floor.
Asked how it goes, he looks toward her: "Hell on earth."

Hilda was aristocracy back home,
a "von," as she reminds the air, before
he brought her here a war bride. Together they hone
the edge of memory to wound each other,

this couple who possess the gift of language.
Outside, rust-spotted eggs have cracked open,
and inarticulate wide mouths clamour
for dead insects which they will eat and turn

to blue-black feathers fringed with orange, the beauty
of burning coals. Their wings will print the air
with swooping signatures of the unlettered,
too short-lived for hope, too short-sighted

for hopelessness. If unlucky, one or two
(blind to glass) will end their lives across
the street, where tall factory windows sweep
bare floors with unfathomable tides of light.

FINE THINGS

"These be fine things, an if they be not sprites.
That's a brave god and bears celestial liquor.
I will kneel to him." – *The Tempest*

1.
A few twigs the breeze has caught red-handed
keeping secrets – tiny fistfuls
of spring ready to burst – quiver, and so
nod to the radio's warning:

an angry wind will strafe this north casement
with ice pellets at dusk, then storm
the canvas of the night's tent, shredding it
to white tatters.
                    But now the yard

sits in the palm of a quieter god
the power of whose focused thought
transfixes every inch of ground with light.
Light pits the empty birdbath, drills

along fenceboard channels the paintbrush missed,
and sinks small, diamond-shaped ravines
in the bare maple's bark. It turns the glass
in the neighbour's recycle box

to green and amber gems, bottles refilled
with spirits of celestial proof
so strong one sip forces the thirsty eye
to water down what it drinks in.

2.
Our neighbour, having had enough of storms,
and having drunk enough last night,
sleeps through this sun-storm. Let her sleep. Her eyes
have had more than enough of water.

After a weeklong nightly squall of voices
so shrill it swept through two brick walls
and the long yard between – after their door's
thunder when he slammed out for good –

she came to our door: did we have a bottle
or two? Some unexpected guests . . .
We nursed the lie, because we had each other,
and gave her wine to take to bed.

3.
Tonight's storm won't last long. The spell it casts
over the greening beds will melt,
and the same god who grips the world this morning
will drink the birdbath's cupped snow dry.

His is the power that will put the leaves
back on the maple, and call up
red-throated southern birds from sleep, to come
in pairs and build their songs on it.

It is the same power that keeps the night's
gems circling on unbroken chains
more fine than anything on earth. It is
the power we would have love have.

Guardian Moon

Circle of sleep at the foot of her bed,
a satellite of her own dreaming body:
    when the drawn blinds' spill of city nightglow
silvers his fur, Lucky looks most like Carol's
    private moon. Which he's been since she found him.

She'll never tell all about that night, its start
    drenched in mute shame as Lucky in moonlight.
What made a loving mother, sleepless for fear
    her husband might track them down, leave her kids
unwatched and wander out to the unknown street?

    Some horizontal gravity pulled her
to the landing – where she thought she met a ghost.
    Her moonlit face in the back window's glass
became her mother's as she'd seen it: sleepless,
    lapped by TV's secondary moonlight,

a statue of ice rigid in her armchair
    the long nights after Carol's sister Meg
was killed. Yet, this night's light didn't flicker. Calm
    promising deeper calm, it cupped her face
the way a lake floats you above its still depths,

    and then its shaft cradled her down the stairs
out to the street, thirsty for the gleam's distant
    source. Outdoors, light had paved the opposite
sidewalk with moonrock, but her side lay shadowed
    by her own building, so she crossed to see

a moon not round but oval, seedlike. She looked
    long, as if her looking might make it grow,
and told, so still she didn't once move her lips,
    her stories to that face: pockmarked, dwindled –
a sister's, wasted like hers by grief and rage.

The story of her mother, who'd escaped
with two daughters from a life of nightmares in
    the city, only to lose the elder
to her own worried eyes, too heavy with work
    as she drove along their sleepy sideroad.

The story of the younger, left so alone
    she tried to make her body fill the space
of two, and when her mother still looked through it,
    tried to make it slowly fade away and
stopped only after her mother's faded first.

The fairy-tale story of the same child,
who married a man who was a prince before
    drinking turned him into a beast that chased
its own offspring, till their mother fled with them
    back to the city hers had once fled from.

She knew the moon would understand – broken and
    knitted whole again, battered survivor
of endless middle-of-the-night departures.
    Held frigid like her, lost for long spells, but
soft-stroking, never withering in its gaze.

She'd needed to have – there, outside herself –
all that she felt she had inside, but never
    could be certain of unless she saw it:
unearthly peaks and hollow spots, the ocean
    of storms and a sea of serenity.

Yet now, with the moon's face propped above her roof,
    her heart called out to it for something more,
for proof that wouldn't fade along with the night,
    some breathing daylight moondust she could touch.
As if in answer, a shawl of silver fur

    unfurled across the street next to her door;
and when it rose and faced her, two pinpoint moons,
    lesser but brighter orbs, shone steadily,
beckoning. She crossed back over, and – this was
    the strangest part, life living its own dream –

although she'd always been afraid of large dogs,
    she let her fingertips lose themselves in
his neck's thick bristles; and, like a sleepwalker,
    he glided alongside her up the steps
and all the way to what became from that night

    Lucky's bed. The children named him Lucky,
first for their luck in finding him, and later –
    grown older – for his luck in finding them.
Yet, most of all when the distant moon is lost
    in night, Carol knows she's the lucky one.

THE HAMMER

The mother whose hand trembled with his soft pounding inside her
    abdomen, marvelling that a complete new being could be contained
        within her,
whose hand guided to his mouth the first small spoon of food that did
    not come from her own body,
whose hand enveloped his hand as her body had once enveloped his on
    morning walks to the building where she would deliver him again,

would not as I have done this morning walk staring past the outstretched
    upraised dirty hand that juts like a downspout from this building,
would not have marvelled even so at his ingenuity in fitting himself and
    all his worldly goods into a diagonal niche between two storefronts,
but would look down at her own hand, beyond marvelling that such a
    miraculous contrivance could clench itself into a thing, and pound
        and pound.

Sleepless. And again the beak, like a hooked hand
pulling out stitching, plunges into the fabric
    of soft white underbelly fur, unravels
the coiled and wet red thread of rabbit intestine,
    and snaps it up. The flashback kindles to flame
so many times on the screen of his closed eyelids,
    Martin wonders what sort of damper it takes
to smother fires in the mind's eye. Science coming
    easier than sleep to him, "operculum"
surfaces, the platelike flap he shows his classes
    on snails and shellfish – glue that, once secreted,
fits like a lead slab.
               Nothing so solid needed
    that morning to shield Lucy's eyes on their walk,
only his hand across them after his own eye
    caught the vulture at work on the jackrabbit
she'd hopped along behind and named the day before.
    "Keep your eyes shut now" – a game, but not for him –
"and tell me how many instrument sounds you hear."
    It worked. The scratchy percussion of their feet
scuffing the gravel, the roadside creekbed fluting,
    the frog's plucked bass-string and the bowed, ear-tickling
cicada crescendos kept her distracted from
    poor Twinkle being gutted by the vulture.
Lucy saw nothing. "Mommy, Daddy's so much fun" –
    her high-pitched solo, followed by the clapping
of the screen door.
              His solo, on their evening walk,

sought out easy modulations – shrivelled blue
tatters dangling where tomorrow bright new windmills
of chicory petals would spin on their stems,
spiders squatting in the house wren's abandoned nest,
ants in the glassy coach ditched by a snake: "Each
takes a turn on earth's carousel" – cartoon soundtrack
of eco-talk reeled off to be rewound in
his students' notebooks. A half-truth. No, a half-lie,
and not so much dreamed up as fallen into,
instinctively. One track in a formatted brain
led vultures to target roadkill and, immune
to the pain, see only food-source; another led
teachers to keep innocent eyes from reading
painful lessons about sudden, bloody spoilage
scrawled on the garden path.
                              A cry. It pulls him
into his daughter's room. Her sleeping eyes quiver
beneath their lids, her lips frown for an instant,
then unfrown as her arm finds comfort in the soft
acrylic fur of Teddy – whose open eyes
stare blindly, unmoved as a vulture's by either
her nightmare or his rescue of her from it.
Yet, Martin thinks, how little of warm-blooded life
can see through the lead shield of its own instinct
and smart, imagining the hurt of another.
A rare gift, this biological given,
but a hooked one – keen eyes make the stinging sharper.
No wonder tears well up in the same small cave
where scenes flicker on the wall.
                              Yet wasn't he,
by shielding Lucy from the roadside nightmare,

stealing her birthright? Gutting her humanity?
    He tries to play the morning over again
without reaching out his hand to cover her eyes,
    and finds he cannot – the imagined horror
hurts more than the real one he distracted her from.
    No longer innocent, he's nevertheless
soft-shelled as she, lacking the makings to harden
    a welling tear into a bulkhead of stone.
How could he – powerless to ward off those dark wings
    that flutter behind shut eyelids – ever have
dreamt of sheltering her from the shredding talons
    that hate or mindlessness or (sharpest of all)
love will swoop down with? The teacher has no answer.
    Now his science might distract or rescue him,
"operculum" being also, he remembers,
    the miniature sounding-board whose trembling
canopied them in the song of the cicadas –
    but unlike Lucy, he sees too much to weave
comforting harmonies from the strains of nature.
    He's wrapped her in the fabric of his thin-skinned
love, helpless to protect her and helpless not to.

The Seventh Star

1.

The uncut carpeting lay rolled up overnight
like a felled tree blocking the hall floor,
transforming their ordinary rounds between

kitchen and living room into new Olympic
events (the wastebasket toss, the coffee hurdle),
or into country walks over collapsed

ancient fences. Even making them laugh.
So now, Anne off to work – indrawn surge
then drum of the downstairs hall door – lingering

he pauses, not wanting to spoil the furled promise
of carpet or of this wakening Saturday morning.
Though eagerness has his hands clipping the loops

of cord and unfolding his graph-paper plan,
his mind loiters in the long coiled bundle
and his thoughts in an instant leap thirty years back

to a rolled-up exercise mat in the gym
of Rosewell Public School; the teacher, Mr. Rifkind,
has just hoisted it overhead as if

it was air or nothing, himself a tall bronze statue.
Where did that image come from? Not since grade two
has Paul seen Mr. Rifkind, probably now

no titan but a stooped pensioner.
Yet, ungreyed still, large as a god in some
heaven where the mind enfolds a child's heroes

unchanged. But now mind catches up with hands,
guiding the measure along the unfurled edge
to where he'll make the first cut in this largest

Valentine present for Anne: one green expanse
spread out like an enormous Raleigh's cape –
the collar to line the hall, the paired flanks fanning

down into living room and bedroom – all
seamless, if his plan works, a perfect wholeness.
A childish charm to make *them* once more whole.

2.
Anne rings up *Pat and Mike* for Mrs. Sztepak,
sees her out, sorts the returned cassettes,
knows she'll find another Hepburn-Tracy

among them – Mrs. Sztepak's latest escape
from six kids. *Adam's Rib*, yes, where the couple
are both lawyers: another one where the absence

of children comes across as perfectly normal –
not looking forward to, not back on, simply
without. There must be people like that, happy.

Not Anne and Paul, and she knows it isn't just
because they now no longer have what once
they did. Back when their dreams were paper shafts

aimed at the future, even then they felt
the ground of their happiness two-dimensional.
Just them: her films, his jazz – a pencil-sketch

the coming children would realize in depth.
(At last one came, staying only long enough
to darken the sketch with small, difficult breaths.)

Was that their crucial mistake? Then, building their lives
around an absence; now, trying to cover
it over, like Paul, or trying to retrieve

a presence from it. The shadows you bow down
before with gifts, or flee from: cloudy will-be
or hollow was, never a solid now

under your feet. She holds up *Adam's Rib*.
Mrs. Sztepak, as usual, totally caught up in
the story, hasn't rewound. She leaves it as is.

3.
He's botched it. Probably no one will come across
the seam he's made in this thick twist, where the joists
sag around the bricked-up mantelpiece,

but he'll know. And how can he make a present of
something not right to begin with? The wave of disgust
peaks as he finishes tacking down the rug –

thinking of how to tell her – and then subsides,
overcome by the simple, practical demands
of cleaning up in time; yet he wonders,

while feeling guilt for not feeling guiltier,
at the mind's changeableness, its agility
in shifting each scene's intricate furniture

along with the scenes. How even the heaviest piece
thins, shot through with mist, lifts bodiless,
and – though an edge can still turn sharp or bruise –

fades into blurred backdrop. The way old letters
on the awning flap of the little restaurant
where they meet for dinner every Saturday

spell out The Seventh Star in whispers under
the shining red sign of The Budapest Diner.
Which they've called by its old name ever since Anton,

the owner, told them about the seventh star:
Electra – eldest of seven beautiful daughters
of Pleione and Atlas, all transformed

to ring the night with their unearthly splendour.
Six diamonds and lost, shadowy Electra,
"the one you can't make out but never forget."

4.

The Captain Video door clicks locked behind her.
She walks along St. Clair, toward The Seventh Star,
shop lights just tinting the pavement at this hour.

The red neon of Cinderella Hair Stylists
softens the concrete into raked pink sand,
and Retro Café's strobe, from across St. Clair,

has the crusted snowbank shimmering like a wave.
Nothing stays put: the sidewalk's transformations,
she muses, match the slower changeovers

of the shops themselves, Buy & Sell clearing out
for Yam's Chinese, Da Maria's hanging plants
filling the window where, a few months past,

upright skis criss-crossed the neat stacks
of handknit Finnish laprugs. Little movie sets,
each (conceived as if it was going to last,

forever holding the shape of someone's dream)
hardly more stable than the celluloid film's
dissolving frames, their weight become a shimmer,

comings and goings hanging in the air.
Yet, the shimmer lingering there after
the things themselves are gone. Not a mirage

of timelessness, like Dollar Discount Store's
perpetual window display of witch costumes,
Santa tiepins, and stuffed pink Easter bunnies,

but a true afterimage. It hovers more
like sound, alive, bodiless in your ear
but real as – no, she thinks, maybe more real

than the ground under your feet. That merely holds
you up, it doesn't carry you clear away.
Like now, at the door of The Budapest Diner, as she smiles

up at the awning and at the Valentine present
still to unfurl from Anton's violin:
Grappelli's arrangement of *My Blue Heaven*, Paul's favourite.

Moving Day

"We are happy when for everything inside us there is
a corresponding something outside us." – W.B. Yeats

Hers gone, the weight of his now moved
    like a hidden cataract
through the bodies of the movers,
    over shoulders, down backs,

to plunge through boots thudding on
    wooden stair treads, which groaned
briefly, but held, and like the rooms
    above them, did not mind

the loss. Upstairs, light quickly filled
    spaces left by chairs, headboards,
dressers – all but his bewildered
    thoughts: deep alcoves, bare floors.

Yet, toward evening, when he detached
    a wall lamp he'd installed,
the black leads curled in on themselves
    like a dead spider,

and when he'd removed the mirror
    over the mantel, the wall-
paper behind it like skin
    after a bandage is peeled,

he read in these signs that the house
    knew venom, felt injury,
and sat in the rising darkness,
    as happy as he could be.

it was, their house on the beach, and they were Mr. and Mrs. Rifkind. Not married to one another. Both widowed, Sue by Mike's late son, and Mike (soon after) by Sue's late mother-in-law. Hers the upstairs apartment, his the rest of the summer house he'd winterized for a lost happy early retirement.

Sue liked water because it never
tied her down, never made
claims on her. She would walk

along the beach at daybreak, taking
shoes off for small waves which reached
out to caress her feet and no

sooner touched than drew back, the water
drinking itself in thirst to lose
itself in the colour and shape of absence.

If Mike's soul could have pulled its way
up from wherever it hid and risen
to words, it would have said he found

infinity in the tall clock, the god
who stood unchanged in a self-induced
trance at the foot of the stairs

while around it years of furniture
and mortals entered and left
and curtains and seasons shifted.

Both wanted to hold something of summer, she by staying in the house of Tom's childhood holidays, he by never facing the last season's last drive to the city house alone. Their parts in the house they shared kept them apart year after year, unattached to the place for itself or to each other.

Anyone seeing him running
on the beach mornings before
he drove to town to teach his
fitness class would never,
Mike was sure,
dream he was nearly sixty.

Same time, seven sharp out the door.
Same route, due north along
the shoreline, sun-glaze on
the waves almost masking
the beach's face, that tan
skin gone to creases.

Summer mornings Sue was out
before him, setting her tripod
like a fisherman his nets, to catch
the sunrises her brush would save
in oils over the winter.

She wintered in the camera's
entrapments, making painted
windows of water, fire
tamed in their panes, the flames
a stingless glimmer.

The ice storm forced them together, his woodstove the sole unwired warmth. Looking at one another hurt them both: she saw Tom's eyes in his, he saw grey in her hair. Talking hurt more – too remote to flow, too intimate to keep bottled and polished. Every thought a shard of ice coughed up, scraping the backs of their tongues.

> Her eyes pained at what
> the shadows cradled and the candle flicker
> rocked, as they held his face: slivers of moon
>
> almost lost in his eyes'
> dark waves, the shore of skin around them
> lit from within like wax at the candle's rim.
>
> Gloom-threatened island, fired
> by its own melting. White hot core
> only to be limned by burning.

> > His ears thawed when the logs'
> > rush of whispers rose
> > over the ticking of his house's breath,
> >
> > wood's voice cracking
> > to splinters, wood exploding
> > in waterfalls, years of growth-rings
> >
> > consumed in a spendthrift outpour
> > that shamed his holding back. His voice
> > followed, unloading words for hers to light on.

That night, without touching, they reached each other, finding summer in winter. Did they then, someone not knowing them might ask, make love? Like driftwood, love's never made but found. Yet, someone knowing love might say they found it was their house on the beach, winterized.

An American Dime

1.
After the theft, she knew there would be no
　　detective's knock at the door, no calls
　　　　from claims adjusters – the heart goes
　　　　　　uninsured. Yet she puzzled

over that very lack: would premiums
　　be out of sight, or would proof of break
　　　　and enter in those premises
　　　　　　be just too hard to come by?

You can't walk the investigator through
　　the trashed room of your hopes, let him finger
　　　　the sheer promises hanging torn `
　　　　　　at the sides of a window

or your broken confidences arrayed
　　whitely on the tea tray. Walking through
　　　　her inescapably solid
　　　　　　apartment, she found a new

largeness attaching itself to an old ·
　　loss: an American dime, gone years
　　　　now from its niche on her bureau,
　　　　　　a keepsake she hadn't shared

knowledge of with him, because she was sure
    he'd think it silly; yet she thought he'd
        known or guessed and kept her secret
            in loving conspiracy.

2.

The dime came from their honeymoon – their heat then
    one with the southern California sun
        on Spanish ruins they darted
            into like iguanas

to be each other's afternoon shade. What
    she remembered most were mornings, though:
        waking early from excitement,
            walking to where the rainbow-

arched stone bridge made a perfect circle with
    its own reflection briefly each day
        before water traffic shivered
            the glass. It was an entry

to a garden paved with sky, where brown-edged
    planters held pyramids and columns
        of green whose climbs and plunges met
            in absolute symmetry,

and, holding up a dime – the one round thing
    in her pocket – against it, she swivelled
        a little silver door open
            and closed on it. Unable

to bring the morning river and the bridge
    back north as souvenirs, she'd cherished
        the dime, held to the eye, enlarged,
            as proof, as what you wished on.

3.
He was always running out of small change
    for the evening paper when he walked
        the dog, but dusting, polishing
            the glass, to find he'd taken

that dime, even before she knew the use
    he put it to, felt like betrayal
        of more than reverie, as if
            he'd reached inside her and pulled

out the bridge itself. Love, no longer whole,
    still held on, stone-blind, partial for him,
        then heard the dime had gone to call
            someone else, and dulled. Time

made dust. She paused now by the empty niche,
    thinking of the coin with its righteous
        "In God We Trust" propped like a splint
            under the President's chin,

regretting she once mocked the gap between
    that piety and the coin's worth,
        because loss moved her now to find
            in those lofty words a truth .

about what is most real: all unwished, yes,
    it slips from you as a dime slides
        through your pocket's fraying stitching –
           yet nothing more solid

than it will ever let it in. The way
    the dime turned to hold the light of once-
        endless mirrorings, before day
           after day turned them opaque.

An Opening

1.

Their car hugged the rail – part of the river
of cars bridge-borne over the river with
    water's grave momentum, hefted along
as if the play of pedals and steering wheel
    were only play. At midpoint, the tremor
of traffic through the roadway grew so intense –
    the car shivered so – he wondered out loud
what it was like to stand there on the footpath.
    His question cleared an opening, a calm
through which she might have raised a secret hidden
    under the crossed currents of twenty years.
Her answer, "Frightening," showed she chose not to.

2.

It had started the day after Merlin
pounced on the salmon fillet left half unwrapped
    in butcher paper on their kitchen table –
pounced and, although she had turned her back for just
    seconds, bounded through the open window,
hauled his prey across the courtyard, and sat there
    devouring it. What wounded her was not
her loss or his betrayal, but his flamelike,
    untouchable wholeness in victory,
and her envy of it, that pure freedom once
    hers, now not, as if he'd stolen that too.

Next morning, leaving Matthew at nursery school,
    her hand still warm from his, she kept climbing
up the stepped walk – slowly, pregnant, a tugboat
    working heavy seas – to where a level
footpath ran alongside the roadway, under
    the cable's arching takeoff. This first try
brought her only as far as the near tower –
    though even there, when she angled her head
over and stared down the tower's barrel, gulls
    below were flies, and rail tracks were matchsticks.

From then on, each of the three mornings a week
    of Matthew's school saw her farther along
the span, following the cable's downward sweep.
    At last, the shadow of its lowest ebb
eclipsed her own. There at midpoint, hands gripping
    the railing's trembling round, just gazing down
(so far above the water level, whitecapped
    peaks and ravines contracted to hairlines)
freed her, lightened her looking into gliding.

3.
    Like the freedom seabirds cry for, she'd thought
then, too ready to hear the rush of plummet
    as lift. The obliterating road-roar
had spirited her out, the way a current
    of wind teases a candle flame half off
its wick.
            And to say now it had been enough
        for her to go that far while she still could
would leave no opening for either of them.

COMEBACK

Even before he turns the master key
back to its upright starting-point and pulls it
    from the cylinder, Ted is carried back
by the acrid odour, an arrow heading
    straight for the brain's rank, lawless borderlands –
hideout of vagrant memory. Back into
    the furnace room of a childhood cellar
where she'd sent him to clean out the sprung mousetraps.
    Repulsive task: furry, rabbit's-foot-sized
corpses, with spindly pink forepaws reaching out
    as if in prostrate prayer – the trap's red-letter
"Victory" too pathetically lopsided
    but for the rancid smell, which evened things:
denied all chance to run or cry out before
    metal oblivion came down on them,
the mice, with one last, lingering effort, filled
    the air with edged, stinging hatred for what
had killed them; so his eyes would water – not from
    pity or sorrow, but because the smell
had wounded them.
                        So, even before Ted finds
    the body, he is weeping now, knowing
that she, long taken aback by the disease –
    shrunken to the small girl he'd never known,
her grown-up jewellery given to daughters,
    her long white hair to chemo, her malice
crushed – had regained the old sharpness, meeting death
    with one last exhalation of contempt.

"... an early closing date, so we'll have lots
of time before the baby's due, and not much
    work. The old folks" – pointing up – "were fusspots.
Once their things are gone, painting will be a cinch."

They sit, daughter and mother, on a red
velvet loveseat under the middle-aged eyes
    of Sidney and Faye (so identified
by the listing agent), painted thirty years
    before, seated on a blue-tapestried
early incarnation of the red velvet.
    While they discuss the daughter's neat pencilled
furniture plans, a gang of renegade thoughts
    breaks from the mother's focus (so deftly
she alone sees it), razors through graph paper's
    paper-thin, squared-off chairs, tables, sofa,
through thick broadloom beneath their feet, not stopping
    until her own first house of thirty years
before looks back up like a flooded basement.
    And while the mother can see both layers
of time at once, she frets at how the present
    thins down to gauze, partly because she knows
the daughter trusts those pencilled lines with her life –
    puts her weight on them as if they were stone –
partly because to speak such thoughts would alarm
    the daughter about *her*. Sidney and Faye
would see it all, she's sure, and suddenly feels
    calmed by his hornrimmed and her scalloped gaze

(that fashion old enough to be alien
    and funny as finned cars to her daughter,
but touching to one who'd lived it, worn it when
    she was her daughter's age, and they were hers).
They'd know. In their mid-fifties, they must have seen
    their children grow transparent – adults whose
large estranged bodies might without warning fade
    into familiar child-shapes – erasures
unthinkable to the children, who assumed
    that people grew toward one shape rather than
through many, and who knew you as the fixed you
    of portraits. Did their children commission
this portrait, she wondered, when the couple moved
    to this, their smaller and last house? And did
Sidney and Faye – unwilling to take it down
    and hurt feelings, unable to kidnap
the children's image of themselves, surrounded
    by its gilt frame – run out at the first chance
and change the tasteful fabric of the loveseat?
    That long-wearing style, the sky's permanence,
to this fragile, questionable red velvet?

A Garden Inclosed

1.

Her mother had always pulled that story out
with the same air of triumphant righteousness
    you might display after uprooting a great
noxious weed that everybody else had missed:

    one of her best moves in the losing contest
to overtake a big sister who marries,
    emigrates, and becomes a mother herself
while back in Chios yours still laces your shoes.

    It was designed to prove that cousin Jeannie's
manic possessiveness was inherited,
    and not acquired when she married Fotis –
fresh from his mountain village, pallid with greed.

    According to the story, Jeannie's mother,
Aunt Daphne, lost her heart to the first Persian
    carpet they could afford, leaving her husband's
bed every night for a week, creeping downstairs

    to stretch out like a cat basking in sunlight
and "make love to a rug" (mother's *coup de grâce*).
    Eleni took up the scene as a child will,
in trust, not questioning backhanded brushstrokes,

and hung it among family memories
where it passed for an authenticated piece
    until this morning, when another Shiraz
at another Daphne's took on such a close

    likeness, it brought the original scene back
to mind – but never to look the same again.
    As if the rain, rapping, pestering her walk
home, entered her thoughts and washed the canvas clean.

2.
    She met this Daphne in the cemetery
last week, while setting some annuals around
    the nearly matched headstones (one more recently
carved than the other, Aunt Daphne having gained

    that ground first too). She'd noticed forget-me-nots
at the next plot before, and wondered whose care
    kept them so neat; so, when she found the woman
kneeling there weeding, she went over to chat,

    although she knew from one look at the outfit –
shabbiness only the wealthy could bring off –
    her own Sears coat would likely raise a polite
border around conversational efforts.

    The first few stumbling phrases met with silence,
until Eleni mindlessly came out with
    what Daphne must have taken for shibboleth,
myosotis, highbred and botanical.

(A word she – far from Daphne's garden-book Greece –
had learned in a yard on the Danforth behind
    her father's store: first heard as *meo-so-tís*,
in common, uncultivated mother tongue.)

The word bridged the ravine between the Danforth
and Rosedale – an invitation: come and have
    a latté, take some cuttings from the garden,
such a coincidence your aunt was Daphne.

3.
    The other coincidence she owed the rain,
a grey wall that built overnight and closed off
    the garden, moving their morning coffee in –
to the waiting minefield of a rug's still life.

Was it the very same? As soon as Daphne
left for a moment, she knelt down to finger
    the lower right-hand segment of vineleafed frieze
encircling the central scene, a flowering

urn that erupted in great sprays of blossom,
filling the medallion's field with pink-centred
    starbursts, white-petalled, blue-petalled, all of them
interlaced by a network of golden veins.

She probed for a break in the frieze – a defect,
her aunt had said, that only enhanced the worth
    of a handwoven piece – but the more she looked,
the surer she grew: this was not the Persian

that Fotis had sold after Aunt Daphne's death
to buy his Porsche. More intricate differences
    than the small gap came back to her, along with
the reason she had treasured the floral scene

    on long Sunday afternoons as a bored child:
how it had given her a place to wander,
    fingers and mind roaming through thick-piled leafage
to lead the little birds trapped in the borders

    through the break, back to the heart of the garden.
As she sat now, borne back in time on this rug,
    Eleni thought about another carpet,
and Daphne, returning, found her close to tears.

4.
    That carpet came from a still older story
told by Aunt Daphne, of the Greek exodus
    from Smyrna. Daphne, parents, baby sister,
and one precious carpet hurriedly rolled up,

    hurtling along in a nighttime procession
of wagons seawards. The outskirts of Smyrna
    in flames, the roadside broadloomed with jettisoned
carpets from overloaded wagons up front.

    Their carpet theirs no longer at the harbour,
where they bargained it away for safe passage to Chios.
    So it wasn't greed or pleasure
that called the young wife downstairs to the Shiraz,

her niece now saw, but an uprooted flower's
need for the soil it grew in, childhood's garden
    forever locked behind her. Harder than walls,
the intimate estrangement of her body

    grown someone else. As now, across fifty years,
groping at these vines' impenetrable weave,
    she felt her own remoteness move her nearer
to a lonely girl whose pain no longer lived except in hers.

    Later, walking home through rain
so thick clouds hid the far side of the ravine,
    Eleni saw the outlines of deep yards blur,
distance dissolving the borders between lawns

    into mist. She thought of the two sisters' plots –
the growing oneness under stone privacy,
    the borders overrun with forget-me-nots,
each holding its separate goblet of blue sky.

Metamorphoses

Sam's fingers grip the haft of his father's hammer
where fifty years of grip have stained the oak walnut:
as if Sid, back on weekend leave from the army
of the dead, shakes his hand. Yet, Sam is the one back,
on leave from adult life, Sid and Faye's child once more
by walking into the house he's come home to sell.

Theirs still, for the dead, undistracted by breathing,
can sing the song of possession more intensely.
Their eyes warble it from the living-room portrait;
pressed into the basement stairs runner, their footfalls
release chords louder at each downward step. Here, in
Sid's old retreat, it pitches its claim through the flutes

of tool handles, and the iron fists of the vice
drum it. Which makes the calmness of the butterflies
all the more troubling, wind-ruffled capes and flared skirts
leaden where you look for dancing, their spreadeagled
deadness songless behind the specimen case glass.
Yet, why should they sing of Sid who had disowned them?

Castoffs from the first time Sam had seen them, hidden
in a basement alcove of the big old house on
Forest Hill. Why did Sid keep them there, not on show
in the den with his fanged heads, sawtoothed fins, cased guns?
When did black-no-sugar, won't-dance-don't-ask-me Sid
ever have anything to do with these addicts

of nectar, these addled ballerinas? Faye knew.
"Sidney," she would say, as if only her voice could
reach who he really was, and all other voices
(his friends, his kids, who called him Sid, even his own,
fired into the telephone like a shot) fell short.
She called to one she'd fallen in love with before –

was it the war? – wrapped Sidney up in Sid. That,
and the drab postwar uniform of what you could
or couldn't do as a grown male: no butterflies,
no ballet. Enter Sid, the new-made man, hammer
in hand, handshake and never hug. Until Faye's death
left him wondering who he'd been left alone with.

The house bore witness how much his hornrimmed glasses
took in, in the brief months before he followed Faye:
freshly annotated fieldguides to eastern birds
and wildflowers, the Hermitage on CD-ROM,
his letters that she'd saved, and, under their portrait,
the loveseat he had recovered in red velvet –

newly unfolded petals of a bulb long kept
in darkness. So the breaking glass when Sid's hammer
smashes the case is homage, kaddish sung by the
freeing and freed son of a long-captive father,
each come into his own by this dispossession
when, for a split second, the wings flutter once more.

SHARP-POINTED OBJECT

An hour later his wife will find him there
sitting on the floor of the parking garage,
    and since it's their usual meeting hour
she'll only think it strange to see him like that
    (hugging his knees, staring up at the car)
and won't guess, until he tells her, that he's spent
    two hours following the bright deep gouge
over fender to door to door to fender.

Mostly it's been one of those rivers seen
from thirty-five thousand feet on a long flight
    where you sense that what seems a silver thread
is, close up, an unbridgeable confusion,
    but a few times his eyes have tunnelled in
so deep that the razor-thin layers of paint
    on each side of the gouge loomed like mountains
and the gouge's road stretched endlessly ahead.

What brought him down from office to garage
was thinking about the sharp-pointed object
    that must have, he sees now, done the damage.
Earlier in the afternoon when Matthew
    stormed out of the office, it had glittered
swaying on its rawhide chain, a pendulum
    telling out the story it held onto,
of times so deeply lost they became time's dream.

An ordinary bottle opener,
the bottlecap-end rounded, the end for tins
    a metal claw. Father and son, rueful
but laughing, hung it from the rear-view mirror
    after the first of too few camping trips:
dry humour after a week portaging twelve
    unyielding tins around Algonquin Park.
It hung on for years, mostly in the thickets

    of downtown carparks. He'd lost track of it,
but Matthew must have kept it through all the moves
    that distanced them – the father's steps upward,
the son's retaliatory withdrawals
    from after-school programs, then school, then home.
Which he'd thought of as growth because it freed him
    from questions; like his reading of tattoos
and piercings merely as habits of the age –

    nothing to do with his. When did the tool
become a weapon? Before that afternoon,
    when the latest broken promise became
(surely) the last? When did the fashionable
    mutilation reach back toward a past
beyond childhood, and the eyebrow's silver gleam
    cover a glance that slashed through history
to the sharpened, unforgiving firelit scowl?

SHE GOES LIKE

It's character assassination time
next to Captain Video, at Mr. Game's
arcade. Cool neon surf breaks over them,

green and purple rippling the metal O's
on lip or lobe. They breathe out a clear gas
of words to warm themselves. Ashley's exposed

navel shivers when they start in on Mr.
Spinelli's homeroom and his history classes.
Her mind fast-forwards *You should've seen the bastard*

this morning, stops, rewinds her eyes catching
his in World Civ sliding down her cleavage.
No, too gross: eject. Instead: "His clothes,

they're like so Yesterday." Safe choice, that place
half underground, walls papered with dead names,
the living room of all the guys' parents.

There, Ashley wears the name Anton and Eva
fit her into when she was only a dream
in the Budapest whose air their dreams still breathe.

"Elektra." Imagine. Years of getting called
"Lightbulb" or "Hydro" in elementary school
sent her off to Central Tech as Ashley.

She broke it to them slowly. They have a thing
about new things – whatever some Hungarian
fossil didn't invent or eat. Anton's

instrument hatelist targets electric shavers,
digital watches, Japanese violins.
"And Eva goes like *Peanuts butter isn't*

a launch. Cheese isn't cheese unless it reeks.
Forget about sushi." She cringes when they talk,
their tongues caught up on consonants sticky

with foreign memories. Yet tonight, past one,
Ashley won't fall asleep till they come home
(the tables stacked, the door sign switched to CLOSED)

and whisper the old world into her ear,
their breath threading with hers in endearments
like nothing spoken by her yesterday.

Learning Motor Skills

1.
End of shift, but his mind still shifts through stages
    of shedding his ear protectors: steady
pour of silence, then nothing, then opening
    somethings, as if you walked under the small
rain of trees after rain, and every drop broke
    into flower around your feet. But no,
these bloom within, the world's seeds turning into
    sound along the birth canal of your ear.

And how many times must you yourself be born?
    Here Pete knows enough to find the answer
by downshifting: it depends how many times
    you've died. He's also learned that rebirths run
much faster: they're the light, quick pinions, while death's
    the iron wheel bearing down with slow force.
And just to wind such thoughts around gearboxes –
    that's a kind of rebirth too, for this man

once a boy who turned to axles, cams, turbines
    to shut out thought. After six grades trying
and failing to get a grip on inked paper,
    he loved Machine Shop's weighty surenesses.
Motors hummed in their black enamel housings
    like purring stones. Pressure on switches met
with quick, predictable response. Every part
    kept its known shape from day to day – unlike

the blackboard's ghostly stick-figures, or his own
    shuddering "Peter K. Bodman," its floppy
capitals never dragged across a page
    the same way twice. So the machines' rhythms
filled him, and their steady reassurance might
    have made his impulsive heart obsolete,
if the uniquely human gear that moves you
    on as it takes you back hadn't kicked in.

2.

Just like that, he thinks, his thoughts following him
    onto the subway car and shifting back
to turn the shuffle of retreating billboards –
    disappearing with the station – into
flash cards: the ones that made his childhood breakfasts
    indigestible, as Hilda quizzed him
from behind the P&H Lunchroom counter,
    and the ones he held, after Peter's stroke

last year, when the parent became the dumb child.
    In the near-mirror of his father's face
he read the confusion his mother had failed
    to read – taken for wilfulness – when he'd
failed her quizzes. Yet, underneath all seeing,
    he read in his own heart the panic she
must have felt, love helpless to free him from the
    deadly stillness of a mind's stalled movement.

Unlike his mother's, his flash cards awakened
    the sleeping words – unlike her, he'd been schooled

in patience, tending case-hardened workings at
　　Danforth Auto-Tech – and as his father
slowly climbed back out through the loosening face,
　　joked even, Pete relearned one of the first
principles of gears – how they jam unless
　　they have free play, a flow of give and take.

Eleni knew that all along: calm floated
　　on watercourses her hands traced through air
during Peter's therapy sessions, and care
　　rustled under the silks of her laughter.
Now, as Pete rode the Broadview escalator
　　to meet her after work, step meshed with step,
her hands shaping his thought, the wonder of them
　　happy in his hands, the fingers meshing.

"The dust she never sees it, how can she
sweep it up?" So Eva, in despair about
        her daughter, to the other four at the
back table after the customers have gone.
    It might be wrong to call them a quintet,
with only Anton's violin and Ida's
        cello. Better look on them as worried
immigrant parents: although Ida never
        (but for two years) lived more than a few blocks
from where she grew up, she feels the neighbourhood
        another country now; and although she
never married and had children, she's become
        the single parent of the child she was.
Best to see all five obsessed with dust, if dust
        is where time hides and is the tongue through which
it speaks to us. This morning, Ida heard it
        whisper through its absence in the classrooms
that held all the days of her life – the childish
        hour, the two years abroad that passed in
minutes before her mother's illness called her
        home to the long afternoon of teaching,
and now the evening's guest performances to
        children who might have been her grandchildren.
A summer of renovations had replaced
        blackboards with whiteboards and chalk with markers
that sweet-talk the children: where dust, compacted
        into brittle white sticks, had scratched its names
across the panes of night, now wands laid ribbons
        of colour on glaze. The change worries her,

she says, not just because it covers over
    the darkness and the hardness of childhood,
but because it robs these children of the joy
    you learn from dust. At eight or nine, she'd take
dust-caked erasers, first thing in the morning,
    down to the yard to drum them on the bricks
and free them from the dead weight of old mistakes,
    clapping sentence fragments and cancelled sums
into a snowstorm that rode off on the wind.
    How can you free yourself from yesterday
if you don't see it, right from the start, as so much
    dust to be swept away? The others nod,
having breathed and coughed up dust from their cradles,
    Anton and Eva in the rubble left
by Russian tanks in Budapest, Maria
    and Salvador in the dust of old saints
they wore on their foreheads every Ash Wednesday
    even before Chilean politics
made new ones. So they all toast dust with a last
    sip of anisette before the taxi
comes to take Ida home. She and her cello
    join them every Friday for dinner and
the music of duets and conversation,
    then she goes back to her apartment for
quieter heart-to-hearts with cello and bow.
    Even at sixty-two, overweight and
pale, she'd blush if you suggested her cello's
    wooden bell of ripening silence held
some of the fruitfulness time had stolen from
    her body; but when she plays it the dust
in the air around it quickens in tempo.

SALVADOR'S TABLE TALK

He refuses to eat in silence
    even when alone
because, he says, it is all
    otherwise earth:
from the tile floor's hardened
    earth to the table's
wood, once rooted, earth-fed,
    to the stoneware's
fired and polished earth, holding
    earth's offerings
caught at the top of their arc
    of growing-from
to rotting-into. Even
    glass, an essay
at spirit, sand incinerated
    clear as water,
breaks and goes back to earth.
    Only words
from the spirit's unearthly cellars
    pour out,
leave no stain on the lips,
    and float in air.

Because he thought he'd learned
    about words at school
and learned otherwise in prison
    in Chile, he talks
about words not as craftsmen

            flourish tools
but as a grandmother leaning
        on her children,
his words the children of his breath.
        When he was stripped
of paper, cloth, metal – all
        earthly possessions –
the words that had passed through him
        as children
pass through their mothers, never
        to be owned,
came back. They furnished his bare
        cell, they hung
the world within its walls, salvaged
        from lost convoys
of thought. They brought him
        himself.
                And with
his wife, at last allowed
        to visit, words
reached out where hands and eyes
        could not, through
the thick screen, to embrace
        her movements, stroke
her sorrow, take her words'
        hands and dance
slow steps, that in the dancing made
        the floor they danced on.

Freedom to come to a country
        of another tongue

was a prison whose stones were worn
     as a robe.
Yet, since the hard foreign words
     were sharp enough
to cut, he picked them up
     (slowly, paying
for some in blood) and chipped at
     the stones with them:
their pointed consonants
     tapped pockets
of air to fill his chest;
     north light, peeled off
edged vowels, unveiled him stone
     by stone, until
he made his way unburdened.
     Owing these words
breath, sight, the footloose
     lift of his instep,
he celebrates now at table.
     His hands,
launching the words, keeping
     the phrases aloft,
will not let them down.

ACKNOWLEDGEMENTS

Earlier versions of some of these pieces appeared in *The Antigonish Review*, ARC, *Canadian Literature*, *The Fiddlehead*, *Grain*, *The Malahat Review*, *The Paris Review*, *Prairie Fire*, *Southwest Review*, and in *Near Finisterre* (St. Thomas Poetry Series). Thanks to all the editors, and especially to David Kent, Richard Howard, Ross Leckie, and Peter Sanger, for their acceptance and encouragement.

"Night Thoughts" was awarded First Prize in the Petra Kenney Poetry Competition in 2003. Warm thanks to Morgan Kenney and to Molly Yeomans for making the experience so memorable and for hosting me in London.

I want to express my profound gratitude to Don McKay and Stan Dragland for their friendship, their care, and their confidence in my work, and to Stan for his inspired and meticulous (rare combination!) editing of this book.

These poems have benefited from the keen but patient scrutiny of the Vic writing group, particularly this time round from suggestions by Allan Briesmaster, Al Moritz, Leif Vaage, and Carleton Wilson. For more than a decade now, the group has provided my muse with steady nourishment and guidance, an incalculable gift.

Finally, where would I be without those dear relations and near relations who have generously shared their stories and their lives with me? I owe so much to my family and also to our friends Bert Almon and Olga Costopoulos, Jane and David Atkins, Harry and Sandra Blitstein, Don and Heidi Coles, Larry and Susan Ioannou, and Anne and Abe Katz. And above all, as ever, to Julie.